**Written and Sung by
Ruthie J. Curry**

JESUS, The Greatest Gift to Everyone

A Song Based on Luke 1:26-32, 2:1-16, Matthew 2:1-2, 10-11 and John 3:16-17

**Musical Arrangement by
Mark L. Maraan**

**Illustrated by
Nidhom B. Muhtadi**

JESUS, The Greatest Gift To Everyone

This song is based on scriptures from the King James Bible.
Luke 1:26-32, 2:1-16, Matthew 2:1-2, 10-11and John 3:16-17

Copyright © 2024 Ruthie J. Curry

All rights reserved. No part of this book may be reproduced or transmitted in any form or by any means, electronic or mechanical including photocopying, recording or by any information storage and retrieval system without written permission of the author except where permitted by law.

Permission granted by the author to reproduce the word search page only.

Illustrations by Nidhom bin Mutadhi © 2024
Musical Arrangement by Mark L. Marraan © 2024
Lyrics written and sung by Ruthie J. Curry © 2024

First Edition

Printed in La Vergne, TN

Library of Congress Control Number: 2024921634
ISBN 979-8-9894301-0-9

www.ruthiecurry@gmail.com

Dedication

All Praises to God! I thank God for the inspiration to write this song rendition about the birth of his one and only Son, JESUS. For through him, all can be saved. I dedicate this book to all of my family and friends. I love you all!

Listen children and you will hear...

about the birth of our Lord and Savior, JESUS, so dear.

An angel told Mary that she would have this baby.

for to be taxed, a donkey was with them.

But a stable with animals and straw there within.

Shepherds were watching over their sheep.

It was a peaceful night and they weren't asleep.

for Christ our Savior was born that night, and a star was shining near.

"You will find him lying in a manger...

with swaddling clothes and his parents, and there wasn't any danger."

More angels were praising
and singing then.

Saying, "Glory to God in the Highest and on Earth, Peace, Goodwill toward Men!"

The shepherds left quickly and quickly did flee.

They found the babe, and gave gifts to him. They gave gold and frankincense and myrrh, that they had brought with them.

JESUS is GOD's one and only SON.

He is the gift. He is the gift to everyone.

Word Search

JESUS, The Greatest Gift To Everyone

```
M D Y G L R P F R I Q C L M S
A M C H F G K X S N G O L D E
R N Y I D C L D T N E E S J M
Y R G F A N I M A L S Z T M Q
G O O D W I L L R J H E A E W
M L G V I L X X A S T C B N I
C Y Q S H E P H E R D S L U S
S F R A N K I N C E N S E O E
P Y R R X S F A N G E L V Y M
E J C Z H Z R T Z L L X T V E
A O Z I B E T H L E H E M O N
C S Z R S I N S S I L E N T Q
E E M A N G E R Q T F H R Y K
H P E Z Y J G J U V G F P P X
R H B Z I V D C L D O N K E Y
```

FRANKINCENSE	BETHLEHEM	SHEPHERDS	SINS
WISE MEN	GOODWILL	ANIMALS	MEN
MANGER	SILENT	JOSEPH	INN
STABLE	ANGEL	DONKEY	GOLD
PEACE	MARY	MYRRH	STAR

Acknowledgements

I would like to thank my daughter Daphne Curry for encouragement and helping with the QR code for the song.

 I would like to thank Nidhom B. Muhtadi for his beautiful illustrations, the many edits, and the timely manner in which he completed them.

I would like to thank Mark L. Maraan for listening to me sing. Thereby, creating the musical arrangement, the many edits, and the timely manner in which he completed the song.

I would like to thank my nephew Marcus Jones and Adrian Byrd for helping me to record my voice for the song.

I would like to thank Auriel Byrd for my beautiful headshot.

I would like to thank other family and friends for their encouragement and support as well.

About the Author

Ruthie J. Curry is a retired elementary educator, author, songwriter, and singer. Whether it was teaching, tutoring, writing poems, songs, skits for school or church, volunteering to share stories on Youtube or at the local library, or leading a summer drama camp, she has always enjoyed working with children in some capacity. She has one daughter, Daphne Curry. Ms. Curry resides in the great city of Villa Rica, Georgia.

Ms. Curry is thrilled to share the story of the birth of Jesus Christ, our Lord and Savior, in a way that will appeal to young children and to the young at heart, through song. JESUS,The Greatest Gift To Everyone, is a biblical account of Jesus' birth based on Luke 1:26-32, 2:1-16, Matthew 2:1-2, 10-11, and John 3:16-17. This is Ms. Curry's second publication all with a QR code on the back to scan and follow along in the book to hear the author's inspired song rendition of the story. "I hope that this story will help the young to know about the birth of Jesus Christ, God's only Son, and that through him all can be saved. He is God's gift to everyone!" Look for more books, and songs of positivity, inspiration, and encouragement to come.

See QR code on back
for song by the Author.

www.ingramcontent.com/pod-product-compliance
Lightning Source LLC
Chambersburg PA
CBRC102342090526
'582CB00015B/194